interval

Kaia Sand

Edge Books
Washington D.C.

The cover art was created by Holly Bressler and reproduced with her permission.

Interval was designed and typeset by the author. Thanks to Meg Eberle Ainsworth, Colby Caldwell, Max Smith, and Laurie Knytych for design assistance.

Thank you to the editors of the following journals and anthologies for publishing poems, some as earlier versions, included in this book: *Antennae, Bivouac, DC Poets Against the War Anthology, DC Poetry Anthologies 2001 & 2003* (www.dcpoetry.com), *Ecopoetics, Ixnay, Kalliope, Kenning, Lipstick Eleven, Puerto del Sol, So to Speak, sub rosa: a journal of poetry and poetics* (subrosapress.org), *Washington Review, West 47* (Galway, Ireland), *100 Days* (Barque Press, Cambridge, UK), and *108*.

"Aquifer" was published as part of a chapbook with Mark Wallace's "The Monstrous Failure of Contemplation" under the subpoetics self-publish-or-perish initiative. An earlier version of "cognitive dissonance" also was published in this way; a later version, in *Antennae*.

I am grateful to many people for their feedback on the following poems, especially Jules Boykoff, Carolyn Forché, Susana Gardner, Harry Mattison, Rod Smith, Tom Orange, Carol Mirakove, Beth Charlebois's "Introduction to Literature" classes (Fall 2002, Spring 2003, Fall 2003), Jennifer Atkinson, Zofia Burr, Susan Tichy, and Meg Eberle Ainsworth. Thank you to all the Washington, DC poets involved with the In Your Ear, Bridge Street Books, and Ruthless Grip reading series, as well as to all the sub-po poets.

And love & thanks to my family.

ISBN: 1-890311-14-6

Edge Books are published by Rod Smith, editor of *Aerial* magazine, and distributed by Small Press Distribution, Berkeley CA * 1-800-869-7553 * www.spdbooks.org * orders@spdbooks.org

Edge Books * PO Box 25642 * Georgetown Station * Washington, DC 20007
aerialedge@aol.com * www.aerialedge.com

for Jules Boykoff

& for Joe Sand (1937-1992)
& Kelly Ainsworth (1946-2002)

Just as the infinity spread out before my gaze contracts above my head into a blue ceiling, so my transcendence heaps up in the distance the opaque thickness of the future; but between sky and earth there is a perceptional field with its forms and colors; and it is in the interval which separates me today from an unforeseeable future that there are meanings and ends toward which to direct my acts.

SIMONE DE BEAUVOIR

To act is to be committed, and to be committed is to be in danger.

JAMES BALDWIN

Let us who live
try

CHARLES OLSON

prologue

1.
how to live in the galore
as we pack
purses

feed
ourselves each day

stopgap
the ratholes—
protect the patio garden

how to stretch a bungee
stretch and stretch it
fling it free
and damaging, timing
everything right

we're all bingeing—
united nations be damned;
we need a new sofa

how to pledge more rising
free and damaging
in this field of human
adjustments

2.
though we
thrive while
trodden, vowing
for vigor, no scorn
for longshots—

we are protractedly
worn

and on and on
and now like ourselves
occasionally, wrung thin
as meted urbane
promise, but
we can be exceptional
exceptional
as water is

we are the whereas, nimbly
the *nines*, cognitive
dissidents, and everyone
is seditious

i.

aquifer

forecast

for a time
a fox remains
   a fox
      a deer
a deer
      then decay
the fox is all
foxes
    all deer

*

not quartz
   movement
then
     not atomic
clocks
     but ruins
tell us time
   or poinsettias
unseasonable as weather
now is

*

while
we title our
meaninglessness
war

*

shadowed by a
government not ready
for action
     but acting
now
     though we hover
like weather around
a mountain

primer on complacency

stay in the florid calm. beyond the crisis
of a car alarm.

move on move on

escape to torpor. cashcrop
their gardens.

affect patriotism. summersault swimmingly.

say 'oh dear.' home your american
dream. title this poem. find closure.

lose pamphlets in the mail. in this country.

say: 'I'd prefer to go on
being. just being
in the ceramic darkness.'

now I've said this
and I'm done.

Cognitive Dissonance

HOMAGE TO OUR CRUTCHES

Grandmother learned to be hopeful because so many people die, so now she says of the president, she says at least he hasn't turned to liquor. Halfway to nowhere I panic, mapping rote maps again, charting as a way of seeing beyond my range.

I DON'T KNOW THE NAMES OF THE WEAPONS

If only we could dematerialize, be an aura for a while. The lingerie saleswoman says you should never tape your giftwraps. If I tell you the contents of my day I feel like I'm balancing a checkbook. Here be dragons. But I can name some weapons like our doing as our undoing.

WHAT I LIKE AND DON'T LIKE SAID THE SUPERMODEL

Let me tell you the story of my body. Chapter one is my left arm. Chapter two is my navel. Did I mention my prologue, my fore-head, my soul? Let me tell you the story of my body said the dying man. It's useful to read my body. It's not a temple or a house or an aggregate. My body. It's an ecology, an elixer, a habit. Changing schools, jobs, changing matter. Let me show you my body said the dying man. The problem with consumption is it's rather embarrassing to own all these filigreed pedigreed bees.

Legible T-shirts

The truckstop owner went winetasting on Tuesday. He's generous
to children's charities, but a diet of corn chips left him anemic.
Junior served a tennis ball toward the sun after too many bloody
marys for breakfast. Chapter three is my bum hip.

We could festoon the golf course with lanterns now that the lawn
mower's broken. To write about golf is to write about fountains in
Tucson. I don't like your t-shirt, but your watch is louder than
that.

In the Corner, a Shrunken Schoolmaster

Let's watch baseball, watch Ichiro lift his bat. Maybe at the end of
life sport is most beautiful. The lingerie woman said everything
should unfold like a Hollywood ending. Please teacher please teach
me. Please teacher please please me. I don't know what to impart.

Babyland America Themepark America

And anyway, if Luis stole a clarinet, next we ask *why*, not *war on
drugs, war on terrorism, war on colleagues*. Our names populate a
list. Besides, chemical weapons are stored in Umatilla, besides, a
little pep coats bitter talk nicely says themepark america rapideye
hysteria, senators etching dogtags for other people's children.

STUTTER OUT THE TEARGAS

Without a face it's not a clock. I'm as calm as an umbrella. How do I shrug this empire off my shoulders? Landlord to my tenantry. Inside the long shadow of a van.

CULPABILITY OVER COCKTAILS

An equation of forks and knives. The tea is overdue. The question oversteeped. The remedy overstated. Howling is happenstance. Grandmother is gorgeous.

Here is my palm to read said the dying man. Why don't you test your prescience? Here is the daily news. Let me give you a hand.

LIFE ISN'T ALWAYS SO DRAMATIC

I overheard Grandmother say maybe tomorrow museum installations will provide answers. Or at least references to the disembodied disengaged language I'm trying to forget. Language. I'll speak in digits. 2 0 2 4 5 6 1 4 1 4 9 1 1 8 0 0 5 5 5 1 2 1 2

Self-Portrait in a Passport Photo

Today I am the tallest
I have ever been

Now I know how it is
with a cup to the ear of thunder

Now I know how it is to crush
dainty books, do penance,
fast on chatter

From this height, I can hold the moon
close like a hat

I am the tallest I have ever been

I wish to postpone
last month's appointments, understand
the sun, apologize to all
the other countries

I frisk myself, policing
the pickpocket, delighted at all
I confiscate

Appellation

he said in my native
language he said in my Zulu
language your name means home
take residence in your name

she said it's what we say to parrots
like pollywannacracker and
Amni said it means coconut jam

or firehouse or ganja or according
to my father dirtyrottenfish
and people say I know
a dog named your name

Gertrude Stein said poetry
is nouns like saying the name
of the one you love
over and over

we say names so people
turn to us and then
we are hundreds
of names we are stutters
of names a reverie

I can make a house like a poem
words are nothing but poems
but I can't pay rent with a name

sometimes words all together
are rhetoric and sometimes
that pays the rent
but I'm tired of anomalies

what are role models
but anomalies

he's such a good role
model because he's
the exception he left
his neighborhood he made
good to be an exception
means everyone else is left
in the neighborhood

this role model
business is tiresome

we say his name and all
his fortune and hurrah
to his compromises or promises

to a community that is many roles
many names this stammering

f e e d b a c k

but

we have less
than a necessary
stockpile or
we're in the lower
ninety percent or
there's chores to be done
or we don't have
child-minding
arrangements

hush hush hush hush hush hush

my thimbled
touch:

(
oh I have hives or the phone
rang or I'm sorry there's
all this feedback
)

and they may say
family farms fare better
when dropped
into a black box
equation

but we know
vigilance is combative
when we have the time

(

plug the television
with another quarter

the bus is late
)

we're expecting
the future
though we trudge
through the ungainly
though we're funnybone slow

living the
unleavened

(

don't worry about the *hush*
don't worry about this poem
don't worry about the dowager's gown
and her ease her clichéd wealth
)

but everywhere a *hush*
says the cartoonist
the truthteller

Obsolescence

let's tell the V.P. to quit
his shell games

quit your shell games V.P.

but now is not the time to talk about this

we like our SUVs organic and
our shuteyes jammed with jingoism
our doldrums shaped like chevrons

but now is not the time to talk about our loudmouthed supply

our painted cake pie
in the sky

now is not not the time now is not the time

the V.P. saw *pinwheel*
when he heard *windmill*

this abundance a decimation
this *unstoppable as we*

this loudmouthed supply
yellowcake pie
in the sky

Aquifer

Everyone winds up
part in the water supply

BUCK DOWNS

without a river
is it a delta
where the Cocopa are
the people of the river
patient as an aquifer

a river takes your problems
says Edna she says
she can't holiday
but she can bus
to the Potomac
we can give the river our problems
    we give the river problems

six billion downstream

we come to Las
Vegas to witness
mirages we don't
come to worry
about water the water
the Cocopa never see
return to the sea

if all the named would wake
their namesakes with adoration

rolling toward blackouts

maybe because of march
madness maybe something
in the water

something in the   lassitude

no

no not

the *yes* and *no*
of flood and drought

———

flood and drought drought drown soak
parch soak parch parch soak
heat stroke killed one worker each day of dam construction

sorry I'm shortsighted or
earthquaking beneath the dam tour sight of our ability
the alignment of planets recorded the day of the dam's christening
salmon after salmon crushed under the alignment

or environmentalism is not about
parklands only or sorry for
this western confusion
as if jobs and owls
in this pitted locale

the spotted owl
an emblem of privilege
I couldn't quite defend
ashamed of this but
my uncle logged and loved
the owls and another knew the fish
levels in the river

who says be patient scholarly and be patient
as an aquifer

as a rout of faces
pressed against hatchery glass
king salmon and we pander

washed ashore in tremendous numbers
we are fugitive
we have nothing we are lent everything

coho pink chum sockeye chinook
a place where wild salmon meet scatter
so rapid spruced in decadence
sonorous neverminded

I desire him as a river
moves to pass a dam

intimacy of small
letters leaning
on each other
an *i.e.*

          my brother and I
lived by a reservoir
at the base of a volcano
where electricity grids

the pungence of burning in under western

intoxication
to make deserts bloom
Las Vegas guests
Los Angeles brightlights
like a funeral to *engineer*
dryness out of existence
to engineer wetlands
where orange trees might grow
to engineer noxious nothing
oh dynastic drought oh a dynastic irrigation stopgap

who doffs whom
it all ends
at the triumphant
crowned corporations

'our audacious
servitude'
an eastern has smaller   narrower
'how many diplomas
and powers at the trustful edge
of our start'

I am not ready to abandon
what I have not learned

common in the same range as and are equally resistant to

let this be a handsome
limit we refuse
and henceforth go door-to-door

with water grievances

offstream	industry
	century
water	war

such is the promiscuous notary
everything's official so
don't kiss water
in the signatory countries

open to such any excavations and hardening
of turnabout people whose belongings are
tragedy-solution-closure

cash crop blaze parched acreage
all leering solvency or
standoffish engagement
and a soda pop solution
for fouled water
horses hauling coca cola
up Honduran mountains

three boulders
spaced equidistant
not strewn
as gravel but aiming
toward spires

rocks
paced a child's stride apart
might be considered
a bridge

—————

a bridge anchored
to the undertow of conversation

we range our conversations
like cows too near
too near the sea

oh say fortitude

river the sexy   forests
lining our highways buffer despair

the bishops worry
some seek spa cure

here, my thunderous
precipitation

this government   a drought of sorts

China issued its own
admonishment   *your game for the rich*

I'm working the desert
swingshift and I want a perfect
sierra snowmelt

what flinch is this what

white salt where crops
once were turning
brooks into

the upstream country

defined by negative properties
being no other than a thin body
when the conduit is broken is
in the creek bed
            a crutch   a shopping cart

in this freemarket environment

fifteen minutes at the water cooler so
that private sector involvement can increase
the burden on

a woman
bent over grounds
for early
parched and dirty
removal

the *yes* and *no*
of freemarket water   or rather
                        the *eenie meanie minie mo*

outsourced   love
making   outsourced
needs

each nutritive   cheekbone
made   of this
a strikingpart
diurnal

not   over the dam
not   under the

cataract hurled
headlong hope
is resistance
to soundbites
is pugnacious
encountering
as a desert
slowly read

Army Corps of Engineer onslaught
on roguish rivers outlawish nature

rock scissor paper
water stops the fire fire stops the earth

we're overgrazing our conversations

lest a drop of water be wasted   seduction of Mulholland
mapping salmon fury   seduction of

slow-drip water   faucet smoke
screen   irrigation dupe

as animals are game as water is a resource
as success is capital accumulation

vexed delirium and economic value
are used interchangeably in this monograph
salmon homing
muscles and organs shred as they fast
their eggs healthy as I hope mine are
as the woman must think mine are
who wants an egg

a tree dies into a snag
the snag falls over a riverbed
the riverbed made of gravel
the gravel pushed into a redd by a salmon
the salmon laying her eggs as she thrusts
thrusts against her lover other males swim over
swim over her eggs adding

a remote mapping psychic
muddlement think clearly think
clearly an accumulation of books
read and theories combed
scrap paper consciousness

a duck black sky before the dredging

———

dredging transformed the desert into Hollywood
as the orchards died as Owens Valley dried

I am not ready to abandon
what I have not learned

to refer to alevin
if welfare changes resulting
from umbrage from policy
initiatives from thickness blue

    tell a watershed perspective
        I can tell him we drink the trilling sky
the degradation of forests
salted roads
aquifers holding
baby blue nitrogen

pulley cordwreck behind
dear ones wandering
the dry uninhabitable house

salmon swimming the rivers by smell
leaping dams or waterfalls
if at all possible

perhaps I'll begin by adding up days
to know as salmon know

status   quo scare show

but
no shadows in pockets

every arrival blown
up toward economy

toward the landed
bohemians
aim their ambition toward
the upper climate
is color

grooved gorges
brackish yonder
many mistakes and missteps then and here

out of hand
of our hand

an interregnum of namby-pamby
tripping over realms and differentials

water appropriation
suitcase bribery and the sea a dancehall

we say

let the market decide
who drinks water

watched as we are
standing in a field watching
a train

Madrigal for Jules

after Peter Gizzi's "Creeley Madrigal"

Who are the egrets we eyed
as we feel searchingly
as we reveal

or who is the egret we mark
as we overturn pages
as we learn

how bookcliff's wonder to be fierce
now we lip salute without loss
gesture struck as we are

as red bougainvillea is kisses
of you [operatic bellows]
and redwood stout redwood sorrow

———

What is the bookcliff you climbed
as you forage for food
as you store

or what is the bookcliff you left
as you corral the simple
as you touch

how anthelion's seabright to be heard
now you pledge without restraint
aromatic lovely as you are

as a hand becomes a pocket
of you [harvest touch]
and sunflower strong sunflower equinox

―――

When is the seabright we grace
as we daylight briskly
as we tithe

or when is the seabright we bash
as we river our worries
as we eclipse

how Utah's three gossips to be seen
now we candle without petals
barren stunned as we are

as the palimpsest is constructed
of you [farpost caress]
and ashen glovebox ashen beaches

―――

Where are the three gossips they became
as they sigh for you
as they sacrifice

or where are the three gossips they burn
as they shed dominion
as they erode

how cave's mountain to be found
now it's luminous without sunlight
hidden faces as they are

as a candle wills a match
of you [voice of sun]
and trillium tongue trillium open

———

Why is the mountain we see
as we abacus click
as we arrive

or why is the mountain beyond
as we believe each other
as we disbelieve

how marsh's egrets depart
now we promenade without a stumble
certain as we are

as mesas are an arm's length
of you [aspen quivering]
and sidereal year sidereal awe

cordials

some kind of public
house, warming
hut, citizen's hall

belonging to the heart.

all things which be cordial,
that is to say, which do in any way
comfort the heart.

and that I laugh.

aromatized and sweetened.

casting forms on
night walls, lovely
people, lovely man.
I come to think
my way to the next
day. but tonight,
cordiality, a tipped
glass.

a daughter
I am at the wake.

This Poem is for a Woman I Have Yet to Meet

for Susana Gardner

This poem is for a woman I have yet to meet. How many women I have never met! Like the one who wore my dress before me.

We careen through hours, placing saucers back in hutches, writing wills and memorizing liturgy. Gathering little tombs in apron pockets.

This dress is marked by spilled white wine, mother's milk, the rush of water from a burdened gutter.

This page is marked by women. Sequestered women who hear the sound of paper in the movement of leaves. Incognito faces clear as crocuses in the sun.

Letter to Layla al-Attar

who
among us can imagine ourselves
unimagined?
                    LUCILLE CLIFTON

Layla,
your daughter bombed
blind, you, dead.
Pilots, fouled
by speed, troll
your crescent.

Bound by
bafflement, happy-
go-lucky, we are criminal,
thieving fortunes like
desktop playthings.

My national identity
speaks for me, across
national boundaries,
to the dead
end of this imperialist
fiasco.

suppose the future

were an arrow
as progress is toward
forward toward
marching band
giddy suppose
the man who wrote

capitalists

are like priests

weren't many moneyed

winkwinks
and all dredging
done

suppose the news
the news supposed

to arrive
on every narcotic
calm street corner

it is now we must begin
to gather, it is now, this future
no future, this

ii.

progeny

But it is beautiful to love the world
with the eyes
of those
      still
to be born.

OTTO RENE CASTILLO

of course the stories of aurora borealis are vivid. bells breaking darkness—
toward this, a creation story. in the end

tundra, and you may know the word, *where one cries mother, I am lost*

roses, burning like fanatics, rupture
the sky, and here—
arcing tremor, my vested
thirst for you
bellows—underworld—bellows—hurrah—bellows—hunger

a small fist of might, you do not sleep
as movement toward morning. you are not biding time.

a bow, a curtsy, favorable etiquette, quick kisses, a crop to be tended

we are busy they are busy

a wave, fingers thumbing hair, a conductor's brandish:
you will know a history—

forests, blue-ribbon cows, scorpions, flames
and flames of forest

this is how close I am:

a foot touches ground more than a hand does. a hand moves like a spider. an egg is as true as a seashore

now you are an

anemone one

rise   a steeple

a stone a spine

some
one

treading

a whorl

so lackadaisical
lovely you
and laughter and

a joke an ear a
shiny inner seam

last names
become a body
of water a sediment-
filled dam

lined with trees
parkland regulations

stolen excavations
bicuspid quarry
worry

my sweet
rogue nation
closed-lipped
promise kiss
me this way
misaligned
choices make
for more
wishes no free
trade for you
today

tagged stone, your signature, an echo of here—

before you can be anything, which I so much wish you would be—

a star a pardon a cat's paw quailing. each rereading a practice in speech,
the aftermath of tantrums. as arrival is broken

and strange is the window within, holler away our do-not-disturb quietude

a toast   :   be
chokehold   morning
threadbare   glory
go to land wafts of pikake all
hunger throated sound
                    see   shells
on the ground shells in the sky
hear me   can you   hear me

unleashed noon deadweighs the day and the next. a lit matchbook like a bouquet of beckoning tyrannical dominion and each of us homeschools kind desire. in earnest I say *yes* to you hoping you might discern the danger, our choices available as a field, the many ways we have used a field

voice
instrument vigil
over you down the

wall or write

of harlot sweet of

copper copper copper copper copper
hobby hobby hobbyhorse sandstone
riverbed riverbed riverbed echo riverbed spasm riverbed spasm

that's the language

that's the earth house cycle

field house cycle
voice house vigil

undress me, yes, so I might
present myself in the tearoom, the
when threatened, the *fold my delicate*

cameo on the folio
frontispiece folded low

cut on the bias or hitched
with a belt, full-legged lamé:
my fashioned throes

as if you
could happen,
as if I could
photograph a
wish, hear the
space between
songs, as if the
cry *fire fire fire
fire* were a
mother calling
her child

shadows in the black box
or carcasses hanging seamed mouths
or quivering wrists tourniquet bound
or pomander of diction steady forth street time
or roost on the stonybrook
or overrated august observations
or turn to the stowaway garden
or necklace of reverberation chatter tone

or I would like to say clearly
bells outweigh bodies weighing down bells
ice cube sway so sound says
so clearly incessant chiming

or hush my hand and all its rings
outside is only a city

no nomenclature only lipstick
        where eyes would be
lauded speeches
        vaunted fear
a quiet now

        only sounds of children
displaced from their play
        wellwishes
from Washington
        tethered to a day
not this day

an aerial view reveals
indelible scores of organisms

colonizing their relations
as skeletons break along edges

along scored edges

coconut grove trapped like an island in a hurricane like nowhere but a hole
or fire or phrenetic selfhood or chained doors so we can't leave

here where wind where waves where flames where there's nowhere but

here there is no story and no end but smoke settling as strangers regard one
another

now a burnt sky and house and house and hours of people: while you canvass the silence, daughters play between meal hours, singing names, until they, too, put down their spoons, snapping names in two. in this coffin

afternoon of no holidays whenever will you come

a body like a fibula, like something
to carry home

the croon of forestry seductive
as an upstream salmon

some rhythm to this western
language which you may speak

so much to say *yes*

I know you as the blind know
a double waterfall

as earth erodes
into a lake

you're like rose hips
among briars, bittersweet

bittersweet, we say, as if all at once
we taste the complications
of our tasks and our

cupped hands cannot
contain water

we rack up years of such dictator desire—but no, not a mess
of collaboration; a mess of absent

partners, too much phantom limb walking. where holy lands overlap
immensely, children

throw rocks at the night. we decimate daily. see not the palace but squalor
on the ground. see not the maple branches but roots just as wide

hungry as you are
you say—neglect no
olive, grape, grain
of wheat

hunt and starlink
a cornstalk unfolding

tomatoes and flounder
and potatoes and silk
moths and silken
potatoes

gather—you say

dim, so emboldened, I strongarm the crux of nothing from nothing. bones groping. egads faux fortune. let's not surrender to this where one cries child, we are lost

you stand at the wake
of all meadows, keening
eucalyptus, wind

if the rivers change
to streets you will seek
new materials. to keen
or to sleep—each its own

movement, a choice
of footing

**aside from the
coroner's verdict** or
the slowdown windup
piracy of time

live on. live
skullnear and on
and live on

NOTES

SOURCES FOR EPIGRAPHS: Simone de Beauvoir—*The Ethics of Ambiguity*, tr. by Bernard Frechtman; James Baldwin—"My Dungeon Shook: A Letter to my Nephew on the One Hundredth Anniversary of the Emancipation"; Charles Olson—"The Death of Europe"; Kristin Prevallet—*perturbation, my sister*; Lucille Clifton—"Here Yet Be Dragons"

forecast
Mount Weather is among the Appalachian Mountains in Virginia, and inside this mountain is one possible location of the shadow government administered by Dick Cheney and other government officials since September 11, 2001.

Obsolescence
A *Washington Post* article by Peter S. Goodman credited North Korea's Foreign Ministry with declaring "The U.S. loudmouthed supply of energy and food are like a painted cake pie in the sky." (January 16, 2002: A1).

Aquifer
The Cocopa are indigenous people of Mexico who live at the mouth of the Colorado River. Despite the Cocopa's reliance on fishing and identity as river people, upstream activity such as damming diverts so much water that the Colorado River rarely reaches the Cocopa people and the sea.

William Mulholland served as Los Angeles water commissioner in the early twentieth century. He led such schemes as siphoning Owens Valley Lake 223 miles through an aqueduct to Los Angeles. This water transfer allowed Los Angeles to prosper while virtually destroying Owens Valley.

Some source text comes from *Measuring Economic Benefits for Water Investments and Policies* by Robert A. Young (World Bank 1996); the Oxford English Dictionary; "China criticizes U.S. for child poverty," Milwaukee Journal Sentinel (February 28, 2001: 4A); *A Guide to Familiar American Trees: The Golden Nature Guide*, Zims et al, (1952); and a video series on water produced by KTEH/San Jose and Transpacific Television, 1997. Single quote marks indicate language and misprisions from César Vallejo's untitled poem that begins with the line "Otro poco de calma, Camarada" as translated by Clayton Eshleman. A number of books provided background reading, but among the most influential were *Cadillac Desert* by Marc Reisner, *Last Oasis* by Sandra Postel, *Blue Gold* by Maude Barlow and Tony Clarke, and *Song for a Blue Ocean* by Carl Safina. Thanks also to Carolyn Forché, with whom I shared many formative conversations about the politics of water.

Letter to Layla al-Attar

On June 27, 1993, Iraqi artist Layla al-Attar, her husband, Abdulkhaliq Juraidan, and their housekeeper (who was never named in any news reports I've read on the tragedy) were all killed in a United States missile attack on Baghdad ordered by President Bill Clinton in retaliation for an alleged assassination attempt on George Bush, Sr. These were reportedly the first civilian deaths Clinton was responsible for as president.

progeny

The epigraph by Otto René Castillo was translated by Barbara Paschke and David Volpendesta. The original language (from the poem "Frente al balance, mañana") reads

> Pero es bello amar al mundo
> con los ojos
> de los que no han nacido
> todavía

"of course the stories of aurora": "the word, *where one cries mother I am lost*" comes from Martin Buber's *I and Thou*, translated by Walter Kauffman. In a section in which Buber discusses language that shows relation, he writes, "We say, 'far away'; the Zulu has a sentence-word instead that means: 'where one cries, mother, I am lost.'" My appreciation of this was deepened through a conversation with Mvuselelo Ngcoya.

"undress me, yes": The italicized language is from *Molokini Island: Hawaii's Premier Preserve* by Mike Severns and Pauline Fiene-Severns. Thanks to Amy Hunt.

"coconut grove" refers to the 1942 Coconut Grove night club fire in Boston, where an artificial palm tree went up in flames and nearly 500 people died. Thanks to Tom Call and Xiaodong Zhang for the details.

"an aerial view": Source texts were *I and Thou* and *Molokini Island.*

"hungry as we are": Starlink refers to a genetically modified corn not approved for human consumption but brought to market nonetheless in 1999 by Aventis (now owned by Bayer); Starlink corn continues to contaminate shipments of corn thought to be free of genetically modified corn.

"I know you": This poem is for my mother.

"you stand at the wake": This poem is for Alan Graves.

BORN IN ALASKA AND RAISED IN OREGON, Kaia Sand graduated in 1994 from the University of Portland. Living in Portland in the mid-nineties, she wrote for the now defunct street newspaper, the *Burnside Cadillac,* and, in 1997, started the *Tangent,* a zine of politics and the arts, with Jules Boykoff and their brothers, Neal Sand and Max Boykoff. They have since expanded the *Tangent* to publish pamphlets and chapbooks. She moved to Washington, DC in 1998 and graduated from George Mason University's MFA program in 2001, where she edited the feminist journal, *So to Speak.* Currently living in Southern Maryland with Jules Boykoff, she teaches at St. Mary's College of Maryland and co-curates the *In Your Ear* poetry series at the District of Columbia Arts Center.

EDGE BOOKS

INTEGRITY & DRAMATIC LIFE Anselm Berrigan $10
THEY BEAT ME OVER THE HEAD WITH A SACK Anselm Berrigan $4
ZERO STAR HOTEL Anselm Berrigan $14
COMP. Kevin Davies $12.50
AMERICAN WHATEVER Tim Davis *forthcoming 2004*
THE JULIA SET Jean Donnelly $4
MARIJUANA SOFTDRINK Buck Downs $11
METROPOLIS 16-20 Rob Fitterman $5
METROPOLIS 30: THE DECLINE & FALL OF THE ROMAN EMPIRE Rob Fitterman
forthcoming 2004
DOVECOTE Heather Fuller $10
PERHAPS THIS IS A RESCUE FANTASY Heather Fuller $10
SIGHT Lyn Hejinian and Leslie Scalapino $12
LATE JULY Gretchen Johnson $3
ASBESTOS Wayne Kline $6
THE SENSE RECORD Jennifer Moxley $12.50
STEPPING RAZOR A.L. Nielson $9
ACE Tom Raworth $10
ERRATA 5UITE Joan Retallack $12
DOGS Phyllis Rosenzweig $5
ON YOUR KNEES, CITIZEN: A COLLECTION OF "PRAYERS" FOR THE
"PUBLIC" [SCHOOLS] Rod Smith, Lee Ann Brown, Mark Wallace, eds. $6
CROW Rod Smith, Leslie Bumstead, eds. $6
CUSPS Chris Stroffolino $2.50
HAZE Mark Wallace $12.50
NOTHING HAPPENED AND BESIDES I WASN'T THERE Mark Wallace $9.50

AERIAL MAGAZINE

(edited by Rod Smith)

Aerial 10: LYN HEJINIAN co-edited by Jen Hofer *forthcoming 2004*
Aerial 9: BRUCE ANDREWS $15
Aerial 8: BARRETT WATTEN $16
Aerial 6/7: FEATURING JOHN CAGE $15

Books published by Aerial/Edge are available through Small Press Distribution (www.spdbooks.org; 1-800-869-7553; orders@spdbooks.org) or from the publisher at PO Box 25642 * Georgetown Station * Washington, DC 20007. When ordering from Aerial/Edge directly, add $1 postage for individual titles. Two or more titles postpaid. For more information please visit our website at www.aerialedge.com.